Psalm Prayers

David Haas

PSALM PRAYERS

CINCINNATI, OHIO

Dedicated to Arthur E. Zannoni,
for whom the prayer of Israel
is truly a land flowing with milk and honey.
With love and thanks.

Nihil Obstat: Rev. Art Espelage, O.F.M.
Rev. Robert L. Hagedorn

Imprimi Potest: Rev. John Bok, O.F.M.
Provincial

Imprimatur: +Carl K. Moeddel, V.G.
Archdiocese of Cincinnati
June 23, 1994

The *nihil obstat* and *imprimatur* are a declaration that a book is considered to be free from doctrinal or moral error. It is not implied that those who have granted the *nihil obstat* and *imprimatur* agree with the contents, opinions or statements expressed.

Cover and book design by Julie Lonneman
Cover photograph by Jean Claude LeJeune

ISBN 0-86716-233-3

Published by St. Anthony Messenger Press

Contents

Acknowledgments

There are many people I want to thank. They form the community of believers that embraces me with love and support. Without them my prayer life would be dry and this book would never have come to be:

—my good friend, Dan Kantor, for the solidarity of his friendship. He is a model for me of one who is tirelessly on the spiritual quest.

—Mary Werner, a wonderful friend who has remained faithful through the many valleys and canyons of my own personal growth. She is also a wonderful cantor, and together we sing the psalms at St. Thomas the Apostle Church in Minneapolis, where she is music and liturgy director. I am grateful for her talents, her wit and for helping me not to take myself too seriously.

—Thomas Morris, Sister Roberta Kolaasa, Jim Dunning, Maureen Kelly, Sue Seid-Martin, Jan Viktora, Vicky Tufano, Bob Duggan, Father Ray East, Maurgerite Stapleton—all dear friends and heroes to me. I'm thankful for the partnership I experience with them in their vision of ministry.

—Joe Camacho, Father George DeCosta and the people of Malia Puka O Kalani community in Hilo, Hawaii, who continue to nurture my faith in parish life.

—Gail Hartman for continually being present and

patient with me in the midst of a long journey of growth.

—Sister Kathleen Storms, S.S.N.D., for always accepting me and for her friendship and spiritual insight.

—Marty Haugen, Michael Joncas, Bob Hurd, Rory Cooney, Gary Daigle, Fran O'Brien, John Foley, Christopher Walker and Dan Schutte—all friends and fellow composers—for their immense gifts and for remaining faithful to the spirit of the psalms as sung prayer.

—my dancing friend, Betsey Beckman, who prays with her entire soul and inspires me to do the same.

—Frank Brownstead, whose tenderness and love at times is at the heart of my survival.

—faithful friends Rob and Mary Glover, Barbara Colliander, Andrea Goodrich, Kate Cuddy, John Wise, Michael and Diane Bilich, Stephen and Judy Petrunak, Bob and Jan Batastini, Patricia Stromen, Mary Jane Moore, Pam Cole, Joe and Maleita Wise, Michael Cymbala, Bill and Janet Brown, Bob Stoeckig, Jo Infante, Helen Phang, Sharon and Mark Nicpon, Carol Porter, Bob Piercy, Jim Bessert, Dean Pakele, John Buscemi, Loretta Reif, Bonnie Faber, Michael Griffin, Toni Kerker, Barbara Conley Waldmiller, Kathy and Gary Eittreim, Bobby Fisher and Sister Theresa Torres, O.S.B., whose faithfulness and fidelity is inspiring and life-giving.

I also want to express my deepest love and thanks to

my parents, who lavish me with their unending delight in my life, and to Jeanne Cotter, who knows me well, sometimes far more than I know myself. Thank you, Jeanne, for believing in me and for continually being patient and enduring with me throughout the journey. I love you.

Finally, I want to express my gratitude to Lisa Biedenbach, Father Jeremy Harrington, O.F.M., Diane Houdek, John Bookser Feister and all at St. Anthony Messenger Press, and especially my good friend and biblical mentor, Arthur Zannoni, whose love of the Scriptures inspires me.

"I am here, God;
I am ready to serve you."

—*Psalm 40:7*

From the beginnings of my spiritual journey as a child to the present day, I have found it difficult and puzzling to pray, yet necessary and vital in my life. As an extrovert who borders on obnoxious, I have sought in my personal and spiritual energies to find the "gasoline" of life outside myself: through immersing and engaging myself in activity, in relationships and in creative projects that have an outward and social dimension. "Going away to a quiet place" to listen to God's voice has always been a dilemma for me.

So often when praying, my own words felt contrived or inadequate, and my self-consciousness blocked my entry into a personal and spiritual conversation with the Holy One. Then I came across the psalms, and what a discovery! I could not believe (and I am still awed by it all) how in psalm after psalm, I found my own yearnings, longings, feelings of gratitude, loneliness, fear, joy and so much more. The timelessness of these prayers and the fresh new gems discovered in each encounter with the text provided the most human and deeply grounded rhythm for me to connect to—and still do.

As I travel in my prayer life with the psalms, I am able to be freed from myself, and yet stay honest and true in the human joys and crises that I live and try to lay bare before God. For me the psalms are truly inspired, for time and time again they have become the words I needed when I found it impossible to express my situation. They echo back to me the strength and muscle to continue on the pilgrim path.

The Book of Psalms is a central touchstone for prayer for Jews and Christians alike, and these ancient texts give voice to both the presence and the absence of God in the midst of the human condition. The psalms are gateways into the galaxy of emotions and movements of life. In the psalms we hear the many cries of the human spirit, and the hymns and prayers of joy, exultation, praise, pilgrimage, peace and yes, ecstasy. The psalms also lead us into terror, lament, anger and even rage. They permit us to enter into prayer and even to journey to places where we would rather not go or are told we should not go.

In this book I've collected what I call "psalm prayers," prayers grounded in many of the psalms found in the Hebrew Scriptures. I am not a biblical scholar so these prayers are not intended to be scholarly translations. They are paraphrases and expressions that have come from my own praying, walking and reflecting with many of the psalm texts. At times they go in different directions and reflect my own spiritual perspective. I did not use all one hundred fifty psalms as my source for these prayers; I selected those which spoke most eloquently to me. I hope that you will use *Psalm Prayers* as your prayer book and to supplement your other prayer resources.

Since the psalms are lyrical in nature and my main vocation is liturgical musician and composer, I approached these psalm prayers from a lyrical and poetic perspective. In the context of liturgical celebration, psalms are always sung. Since these prayers are inspired and based on the psalms but are not scholarly translations with exegetical grounding, I advise against using these renderings in the context of communal worship, especially in the context of Sunday Eucharist.

You could, however, use these psalm prayers in the context of prayer in small groups, retreat gatherings, and of course, for individual prayer and spiritual growth. The musical nature of the prayers encourages you to sing these prayers to their own musical chant or cantillation.

Each psalm prayer begins and ends with an antiphon, so I suggest you begin by centering in silence, then pray or sing (composing your own melody or just chanting freely) the antiphon, follow this by another short time of silence, and then pray the text which follows. After praying the text, breathe deeply, taking time for the words to touch the heart, and then conclude with the antiphon again. Feel free to use and adapt these prayers to complement and affirm your own prayer rhythm.

The book provides indexes for the liturgical season or feast, time of day, references for sacramental and other moments, and a listing of themes or areas of special need which the psalm prayers address.

The psalms are an unending storehouse of prayer and spiritual guidance. May they expand the prayer deep within your heart and lead you closer to the wonder and gift of God.

Soli Deo Gloria!

David Haas

The Emmaus Center for Music, Prayer and Ministry
St. Paul, Minnesota
March 25, 1994
Annunciation of Our Lord

Blessed and Happy Are We

Blessed and happy are we
who keep our hope in God.

Blessed and content are all
who reject evil,
who do not honor the ways
of the wicked.
Blessed are all who ponder
by day and night
the ways of God,
like blooming trees
amid the flowing water.
They spring forth
the fruit of the season,
the leaves remain fresh,
and all creation is new.

The lost and the lawless
will be whisked away
by the wind of God;
for God will keep watch for us,
and blessed are we!

Blessed and happy are we
who keep our hope in God.

Adapted from Psalm 1

Lift Me Up

Lift me up and save me, O God.

There are many
who seek to harm me;
many who would wish to see me fall.
They talk about me
and snicker,
"No help will come
to this one from God."

But you are my armor,
my power,
and you lift me high.
When I call out to you,
you send your answer
from the highest mountain.

I know that when I fall asleep,
I will awake again,
safe in your arms.
I will not be afraid of the throngs
who come at me from every side.

Lift me up and save me, O God.

Adapted from Psalm 3:2-7

Enlighten Our Eyes

God, may the joy of your face
enlighten our eyes.

When I call out to you,
I need you to answer me,
for you always come to me
when I am afraid.
Show your compassion,
make it known to me.

I know that you are filled
with wonderful surprises for us
when we remain faithful to you.
You always hear me.

Let your light shine on us!
You have filled me
with a joy impossible to express!

I will always be able to rest peacefully,
knowing that you are with me,
keeping me safe.

God, may the joy of your face
enlighten our eyes.

Adapted from Psalm 4:2, 4, 7-9

12 Listen to Me

Listen to me, God,
and be attentive to the groanings
of my heart.

I call upon you,
and in the morning
I will listen to your voice.
In the early hours
I wait and watch for you.

You do not love evil,
you do not keep company
with those who do wrong.
The arrogant do not sway you,
or influence your ways.

You know hate
only in the midst of sin;
you will destroy all lies.
The violent and the deceitful
are kept far away from you.

But you have invited me
into your home;
I am moved and humbled
to worship you in your presence.

Lead and guide me, God;
make yourself known to me.

Listen to me, God,
and be attentive to the groanings
of my heart.

Adapted from Psalm 5:2-9

14 Your Name Is Wonderful

Your name is wonderful,
everywhere!

I will reverence your name above the skies,
even though my song is like babble.
You have built a wall
too great for your opponents
to avenge you.

When I take the time to look upward,
and see the result of your creativity,
I wonder,
why do you even give us the time of day?
Why do you care for us so much?

Yet you decide to identify yourself with us,
and you adorn us
with the same glory that you wear.
You give us the power over creation
and ask us to put everything
in our domain;
all of the animals and living things:
sheep,
cattle,
all of the flying birds
and fish that frolic in the sea!

Your name is wonderful,
everywhere!

Adapted from Psalm 8

16 **You Will Protect Us**

You will protect us,
we have faith in you!

Come to us,
God,
for no one seems to care anymore!
It is nearly impossible
to count on anyone.
Everyone speaks ill of each other;
they do not mean what they say.
It is hard to know whom to trust.

You will destroy all evil speech,
and we believe in your promise.
Keep us always close to you
and preserve us from this world.

You will protect us,
we have faith in you!

Adapted from Psalm 12:2-5, 7-8

All My Hope Is in You

All my hope is in you;
keep me faithful to your Word.

How long must I wait?
Have you forgotten me again?
Why are you testing me
and keeping your distance?

I keep trying to find a way
to keep going.
How much more am I to take?

Come clean, God.
Look me straight in the face
and give some answers.
I do not want to become hopeless,
so that my enemies
can say that they have won me over.
They delight when I falter.

I have trusted you,
and I rejoice in you;
let me keep singing of your
goodness to me.

All my hope is in you;
keep me faithful to your Word.

Adapted from Psalm 13

18 **We Must Do Justice**

We must do justice;
only then can we see your face.

God,
who are the members
of your family?

The ones who live with you
are the ones who walk with integrity;
and those who keep the truth
deep in their heart,
they speak only what is true;
they do not speak lies about others;
they treat all with respect.

They honor you,
and they do not accept
interest on their loans,
nor will they attempt
to trick the innocent.

If we follow this path,
we will never stumble.

We must do justice;
only then can we see your face.

Adapted from Psalm 15

Show me the path for my life:
for you are my portion and cup,
and I claim you as my treasure.

In you I find safety,
and I sing:
"You are my God.
You are my joy.
You are my path of life."

I bless you,
the one who guides me,
you lead my heart through the night.
I keep my eyes always on you,
and with you I see the light.

In you I will rejoice deeply,
even my body will rest in peace;
for you will not leave me for dead,
you will always keep me safe.

In your light we will walk.
You show us your path,
which is the fullest joy possible.

Show me the path for my life:
for you are my portion and cup,
and I claim you as my treasure.

Adapted from Psalm 16:1-2, 5, 7-11

When You Appear, O God

When you appear, O God,
I will dance and sing for joy!

Hear me, God,
and listen to my cry!
I pray before you in total truth.

I have been faithful to you,
I have not weakened.
I hope that you will listen to me
and lean toward my voice.
Hear me!

I hope that I am still
the apple of your eye.
Please keep me safe in your arms.
I will walk in justice,
and then I will see your face;
upon waking I shall be filled
with your peace.

When you appear, O God,
I will dance and sing for joy!

Adapted from Psalm 17:1, 5-6, 8, 15

I Love You, God

I love you, God;
for you are my strength and my song!

You are the source of all strength to me;
my rock,
my liberator,
my source of all help.
I praise you!
You keep me safe from all harm.

You live!
Blessed be your name,
my rock!
You are victorious on our behalf,
and have anointed us with your kindness.

I love you, God;
for you are my strength and my song!

Adapted from Psalm 18:2-4, 47, 51

22 Your Words Are Everlasting

God, your Word is everlasting!

The laws of God are wonderful and perfect,
bringing the soul to life.
The direction of God is one
that we should believe in,
for all of us,
to the very least,
have shared in its wisdom.

All our hearts are filled with joy
with the paths of our God.
There is clarity in God's command,
and we now can see clearly.

Our God is awesome and holy,
unending is God's way.
The decree of God is true and just.

Your Word is gold!
It is purer than the greatest gold,
more pleasing and sweet
than honey from the comb.

God, your Word is everlasting!

Adapted from Psalm 19:8-11

Why Have You Left Me?

God, my God,
why have you left me?

All who look at me laugh at me,
they mock me,
they say to me:
"This one put faith in God,
let this God come to the rescue."

Many wild animals have encircled me,
a throng of the wicked close in;
they rip me apart,
tearing holes in my hands and my feet,
I can number all of my bones.

They take my clothing,
and divide it among themselves,
they gamble for my coat.
God, do not leave me,
help and answer me!

God, my God,
why have you left me?

Adapted from Psalm 22:8-9, 17-20

You Are the One Who Shepherds Me

You are the one who shepherds me,
in you I want nothing.

The pastures are fresh and green,
you give me rest.
You take me by the hand to peaceful waters,
and you give new life to my soul.

You guide me,
and you are true to your wonderful name.
If I stumble in dark places,
I am not afraid;
for you are always with me
with your staff that strengthens me.

You have prepared for me a feast
in the midst of those who would harm me.
You anoint and heal me;
my cup of joy is overflowing.

I believe that your goodness and kindness
will always be with me
for the rest of my life.
With you I will make a home forever.

You are the one who shepherds me,
in you I want nothing.

Adapted from Psalm 23

Enter In, O God

Enter in, O God;
you are the center of my life.

The earth and all of its fullness
belong to God;
the whole world
and all who live.
God formed the earth
from the sprouting sea
and built its foundation upon the rivers.

Who has the ability to climb
the mountain of God?
Who can stand where God stands?
Only those who keep their hearts pure.

These are the ones who will know
God's blessing,
and God will keep us free from guilt.
If we seek God,
we will find the face of glory!

Enter in, O God;
you are the center of my life.

Adapted from Psalm 24:1-6

26 **I Give My Life to You**

I give my life to you,
for you are my God.

You I trust,
make your plan known to me;
teach me,
help me to walk in faith,
for you are the one who can save me.

You are good and just,
and you teach all who would fall
the way to humility and justice.

Make your kindness known to me
and to all who keep your promise.
If we honor you,
you will show us your friendship
and lead us in the way of your covenant.

I give my life to you,
for you are my God.

Adapted from Psalm 25:4-5, 8-10, 14

You Are the Wall of Light

God, you are the wall of light
that keeps me safe forever.

God is my light,
the light that saves and frees!

I seek only one thing:
to live out my life in God's presence.

I will come to know your beauty
in the life that comes after death.
I hope in you,
I will wait for you,
I will rest in you.

God, you are the wall of light
that keeps me safe forever.

Adapted from Psalm 27:1, 4, 13-14

28 **God Will Bless Us**

God will bless us with peace.

Give to God!
Everyone!
Give with all you have!
Give to God all that is deserving!
Give to God a most glorious name!

The voice of God sounds everywhere,
even across the waters.
The music of God is tremendous,
the best of all!

God slashes the sky with awesome thunder!
All shout, sing
and dance: "Glory!"
God's home is above the raging sea
and leads us on forever!

God will bless us with peace.

Adapted from Psalm 29

You Have Rescued Me, God

You have rescued me, God;
I praise and thank you!

My God,
over and over again
I call out for your help,
and you heal me
and make me whole.

If we are faithful,
we will always sing to you.
Your anger does not last for long,
and your kindness never ends.
We weep at night,
but we laugh and sing with the sun.

Be merciful to us,
for you transform our sadness
into unbelievable joy.
I thank you, God,
always.

You have rescued me, God;
I praise and thank you!

Adapted from Psalm 30:2, 4, 5-6, 11-13

30 You Hold My Life

You hold my life;
forever in your hands
you hold my life.

I bring my pain to you;
do not shame me,
but rescue me
and fill me with your spirit.

All who hate me,
they mock me,
they leave me alone and fearful.
I am forgotten,
like those who die alone;
I am like a broken and lost object.

Come into my darkness
and shine your light;
save me
with the sword of your kindness.
In you I will place my trust
and my service.
Give me courage,
give me hope!

You hold my life;
forever in your hands
you hold my life.

Adapted from Psalm 31:2, 6, 12-13, 15-17, 25

When I Am Troubled

When I am troubled,
I turn to you,
and you are there.

We are so blessed
when we are forgiven;
God calls us "innocent,"
and the spirit is given in good faith.

I came forward
and owned my own failings.
I came clean,
and you took away the shame
that had kept me a prisoner.

When I am troubled,
I turn to you,
and you are there.

Adapted from Psalm 32:1-2, 5

32 **Your World Is Beautiful**

Your world is beautiful,
filled to the brim with your goodness!

Your word is justice,
and your actions
are true to your wonderful name:
"Faithful One."
Your love is infinite,
the well never runs dry.

Your eyes are fixed
on those who are patient
and wait for you.
You will keep us alive,
and we will never know hunger.

We wait for you.
You,
the one who is our hope.
May you fill us with kindness,
as we grow strong in our faith.

Your world is beautiful,
filled to the brim with your goodness!

Adapted from Psalm 33:4-5, 18-20, 22

Taste the Magic

Taste the magic of God's goodness!
Drink it in!

I will never stop singing!

For God is my boast,
and all the poor will listen
and rejoice in my song!

Be joyful with me
as I praise God!
God answered both you and I
when we cried out,
and freedom came forth
from the skies.

Come,
look above,
below,
beyond
and within:
God's joy is everywhere!
God takes our shame,
embraces our pain,
and we feel the release!

Taste the magic of God's goodness!
Drink it in!

Adapted from Psalm 34:2-7

ou Are the Fountain of Life

You are the fountain of life,
and in your light we see light.

God,
your kindness knows no bounds;
it shines forth everywhere!
Your justice towers above like mountains,
and your wisdom is as deep as the ocean.

You are precious to us,
and we are your children,
flying with you in the shadow of your wings.
You lavish us with gifts,
and you lead us to the stream to drink.

Keep up your kindness with us,
and defend all of us who are faithful to you.

You are the fountain of life,
and in your light we see light.

Adapted from Psalm 36:6-11

I Am Here, God

I am here, God;
I am ready to serve you.

I waited for you,
and you knelt down and listened to me.
You filled me with a new song,
a hymn of unending praise!

You did not want me
to offer a sacrifice,
but rather,
to have my ears fully open
to hear your Word.
I cried out:
"I am here."

My destiny is written down,
I want to listen to know your will for me.
O God,
I delight in serving you,
your ways are deep in my heart!

I am here, God;
I am ready to serve you.

Adapted from Psalm 40:2, 4, 7-10

Heal Me

Heal me, God.
I am in need of your healing.

Happy are all those
who are present to the poor ones;
God will bless us.
God will keep us safe
and not turn us over to those
who would hurt us.

God will heal us in our sickness,
and I am crying out as before:
"Heal me, even though
I do not deserve it!"

You sustain me
and allow me to be with you forever.
Blessed are you, God,
forever.

Heal me, God.
I am in need of your healing.

Adapted from Psalm 41:2-5, 13-14

I Long for You

I long for you;
I am like a deer searching for water.

I thirst for you, God,
I long to see you, the living God!
Where do I find you?

Break the darkness with your light;
you have promised to lead me
to the highest mountain
where you live.

Then I will go to your altar,
you, the God of my gladness and joy!
I will thank you
and make music for you, O God!

I long for you;
I am like a deer searching for water.

Adapted from Psalm 42:3 and Psalm 43:3-4

38 Blast the Trumpet

Blast the trumpet for God,
the God who takes the throne of heaven!

Everyone!
Come, clap your hands
and shout to God!
Our God is an awesome God,
who reigns over the earth.

Sing praise everyone!

For God is the one who rules!
God should reign in our hearts,
and we should sing praise!

Blast the trumpet for God,
the God who takes the throne of heaven!

Adapted from Psalm 47:2-3, 6-9

Purify My Heart

Purify my heart, O God.

God, be merciful and gracious,
be compassionate
in the midst of my sin.
Over and over again,
cleanse and wash me.

Purify my heart,
keep the spirit in my soul
steady and strong.
Keep me close to you
and embrace me with your spirit.

Help me to welcome back
the wonderful joy of your saving power.
God, open my joyful lips,
which will proclaim and praise you
forever!

Purify my heart, O God.

Adapted from Psalm 51:3-4, 12-14, 17

40 **I Trust in Your Kindness**

I trust in your kindness, God,
forever and ever I will believe in you.

Like the green olive tree
in the house of God,
I say to you:
"Trust in God's kindness."

God,
I will always thank you
for all you have done
and witness to others your saving name.

I trust in your kindness, God,
forever and ever I will believe in you.

Adapted from Psalm 52:10-11

God Upholds Me

God upholds me forever,
giving my life freedom and peace.

With your name,
save me, O God,
defend me and hear my prayer,
listen to my voice.

For many have risen against me,
they want to kill me;
they do not know you.

For I know and believe
that you are my help;
you are my life.
I will offer my life to you
and praise the wonder that you are!

God upholds me forever,
giving my life freedom and peace.

Adapted from Psalm 54:3-6, 8

42 **Give Your Cares to God**

Give your cares to God
and know that your prayers will be heard.

If I had the wings of a dove,
I would fly away to safety.
I would fly far,
far away,
I would hide in the wilderness.

I would hurry to find shelter
from the violence of the storm.

I see crisis and evil everywhere.
All day and all night,
fear lurks upon the city walls.

But I will offer my fear to you,
and I know you will never leave me alone.

Give your cares to God
and know that your prayers will be heard.

Adapted from Psalm 55:7-11, 23

Rest Only in God

Rest only in God,
for God holds our salvation.

God is the strong rock
that keeps me strong;
I will not be shaken.

Hope only in God;
there is no one else to support me.

God alone is safety,
God alone is our hope,
God alone is our glory,
God alone is worthy of our trust.
Give to God with all your heart.

Rest only in God,
for God holds our salvation.

Adapted from Psalm 62:2-3, 6-9

44 I Thirst for You

I thirst for you, O God.

God,
I am anxious and eager
to find you;
like the dry and weary desert,
my flesh reaches out to you.

I look for you in your holy dwelling,
to know and feel
your strength and power,
for your compassion
is the greatest gift in my life.
I will always sing praise to you.

As long as I can breathe,
I will offer to you a blessing;
I will lift my hands high
and shout your name!
My soul will be filled
with the finest of the feast,
and I will acclaim you!

I will always remember you
at my time of rest,
and I will linger
in the memory of your presence.
For you are the one
who is there for me,
and in the comfort of your wings,
I sing, again and again!
I pursue you
from the depth of my soul;
and your right hand will keep me safe.

I thirst for you, O God.

Adapted from Psalm 63:2-6, 8-9

46 **Your Seed**

Your seed will fall on good soil,
bearing the fruit of heaven.

You come upon our land
and water it well.
Your wellsprings are full,
and you have prepared the land,
drenching all of the furrows,
breaking up the clodding
and softening it with your gentle rain.

You have given us a year of plenty,
your richness overflows the path,
and the hills are filled with your rejoicing.

The fields are clothed well with flocks,
and the valleys are singing for joy!

Your seed will fall on good soil,
bearing the fruit of heaven.

Adapted from Psalm 65:10-14

The Whole Earth Cries Out

The whole earth cries out to God,
singing for joy!

Glory to God's name!
Offer your praise
and say to our God,
"You are wonderful to us!"

All of the world genuflects
and gives you honor.
Come now!
Come and see what God has done!

The sea is now dry land;
the people passed through
the terror of the flood on foot.
Let us rejoice,
for God rules forever!

Listen,
all who honor God;
listen to what God has done for me!
I bless you God,
for you listened to my prayer.

The whole earth cries out to God,
singing for joy!

Adapted from Psalm 66

48 Let the Nations Praise You

Let all the nations praise you;
all the people will sing praise to you!

Have mercy on us, God,
and bless us well;
allow us to see the brilliance of your face.
Make your ways known to us
and show your saving ways to everyone!

Everyone will be glad,
because you rule justly;
you guide all of us back to you.

Bless us, God,
and may we all revel in your presence!

Let all the nations praise you;
all the people will sing praise to you!

Adapted from Psalm 67:2-3, 5-6, 8

The Poor Have a Home With You

The poor have a home with you,
because your goodness is overflowing.

Those who follow you
are filled with happiness;
let everyone sing and dance their praise
to the wonderful name of God!

You are in your temple,
with the parents of orphans
and with those who walk with the widow.
You share with all of the lowly
your wonderful home,
and you set all the prisoners free.

You flood us with your rain from above,
showering down upon your people;
you restored the broken land
and have given the needy a resting place.

The poor have a home with you,
because your goodness is overflowing.

Adapted from Psalm 68:4-7, 10-11

50 **If You Love Me**

If you love me,
then answer me now, O God.

Because of you,
I suffer the pain of insult,
and I have to cover my face in shame.
I am now known as an outcast
and a stranger to my own mother's children.
For I am obsessed with your dwelling,
and if they scorn you,
they scorn me.

Hear my prayer,
for I long to be in your favor!
I know that you are the source of kindness;
have mercy on me!

You are the friend of the poor,
and we are your people;
we believe you will not turn us away.
Let all creation praise you!

If you love me,
then answer me now, O God.

Adapted from Psalm 69:8-10, 14, 17, 33-35

Your Salvation Is My Song

Your salvation is my song,
and I will sing forever!

God, I crawl to you again,
keep me free from disgrace.
Come quickly to save me,
and listen to my prayer.

Be strong for me when I cannot,
for without you I am powerless.
Shelter me from evil.

You are hope when all seems hopeless,
you are trustworthy when I feel suspicious.
I can depend on you as I always have,
since I came forth from the womb.
You are my strength!

I will shout loudly your justice,
and of your salvation which never ends!
You have led me since my youth,
and I will always acclaim you!

Your salvation is my song,
and I will sing forever!

Adapted from Psalm 71:1-6, 15-17

52

We Will Be Filled

We will be filled with justice and peace,
which flows from the goodness of God!

Gift us, God,
with justice from heaven;
may your justice govern all,
and those who are afflicted.

Justice will flow down upon us,
as well as the peace of God,
until the moon fades away;
ruling from sea to sea,
to the very ends of the earth.

The poor one will be rescued;
when there is no help,
help will come.
Compassion will be poured out
for the lonely and weary;
and all will be saved!

May God's name always be held holy!
God's name will always be with us!
All people will be blessed,
and the nations will sing for joy!

We will be filled with justice and peace,
which flows from the goodness of God!

Adapted from Psalm 72:1-2, 7-8, 12-13, 17

You Have Given Us Bread

You have given us bread,
our food from heaven.

We have seen it,
we have heard it
and can claim to know
what our parents have told us:
that our God is holy and strong!

God commands the skies,
and the doors of heaven are opened wide,
raining down bread and nourishment
and leading us to the mountain of God!

You have given us bread,
our food from heaven.

Adapted from Psalm 78:3-4, 23-24, 25, 54

God, Turn to Us

God, turn to us;
we need to see your saving face.

Shepherd of our lives,
shine forth with the power of your angels
and save us now!

Look down and see us for who we are;
take care of the vine which you planted.

Help us with the strength of your offspring,
then we will never run from you;
be born in us again,
and we will sing your name!

God, turn to us;
we need to see your saving face.

Adapted from Psalm 80:2-3, 15-16, 18-19

Your Home Is Wonderful

Your home is wonderful, O God,
beautiful and lovely to the eyes!

I long for you
and for your holy temple.
My heart,
my entire body,
aches for you, my God!

Even the sparrow can find a home,
all of the young find a nest,
where their mother keeps watch.
O, how I long to approach your altar,
my life and my God!

Everyone is happy in your home,
and our praise for you is full.
Shield and anoint us with safety.

I would rather spend one day with you
than years upon years elsewhere;
I do not want to be with the wicked;
I want to be with you.

Your home is wonderful, O God,
beautiful and lovely to the eyes!

Adapted from Psalm 84:3-5, 10-11

Show Us Your Kindness

Show us your kindness, O God.

I will listen to the song of God;
our God sings of peace,
peace to all people.
If we honor God,
we will find salvation,
and God's glory
will find a home in us.

Dignity and fidelity will find each other;
peace and justice will kiss.
Truth shall rise forth from the lies,
and righteousness
will come forth from the sky.

God will send the rain,
and we will have a rich harvest.
Beauty and truth will come
from the presence of God.

Show us your kindness, O God.

Adapted from Psalm 85:9-14

Goodness and Forgiveness

Goodness and forgiveness
come from the hand of our God.

Your kindness is unbelievable;
whoever calls to you,
you respond.
Listen now to my plea.

Everyone,
from all the corners of the earth,
come forward to heap their praise on you.
You are great and loving,
for you are God.

You are slow to anger,
and regardless of our infidelity,
you always remain faithful to us.
Once again,
I ask you to turn to me
and strengthen me.

Goodness and forgiveness
come from the hand of our God.

Adapted from Psalm 86:5-6, 9-10, 15-16

58 **My Song to You Is Forever**

My song to you is forever,
and your goodness will always sing
within me.

I will sing forever to you, my God;
throughout all time,
I will make music to you.
For you have been kindness and
faithfulness
for all generations,
and your goodness is confirmed in heaven.

You have made a covenant
with your chosen one,
and established your reign over our lives.

My song to you is forever,
and your goodness will always sing
within me.

Adapted from Psalm 89:2-5, 27

Stay close to me,
and be with me when trouble finds me.

You who live in the hideaway of God,
who rest in the shade of God, sing out:
"You are my refuge and safety,
you are the one I trust."

Evil will not come close,
no harm will approach your home,
for God has commanded the angels
to keep you safe throughout your journey.

The angels will lift you above all evil,
in case your feet are caught by the stone.

God will save those who keep close,
and all will be protected.
We know the name of God,
and God will answer our call
with salvation from on high!

Stay close to me,
and be with me when trouble finds me.

Adapted from Psalm 91:1-2, 10-14, 16

60 It Is Good to Thank You

It is good to thank you
and to dance to the wonder of your work!

I will announce you to everyone
and tell them of your mercy at the dawn,
and of your constancy throughout the night.

The one who is just
will flourish like the palm tree and the cedar.
If we plant ourselves in God's house,
we will grow and blossom in God's presence.

Even in our aging,
the fruit will be in abundance;
we will remain vigorous and full of energy,
and tirelessly proclaim the justice of our God,
in whom there is only good.

It is good to thank you
and to dance to the wonder of your work!

Adapted from Psalm 92:2-3, 13-16

If We Have Heard the Voice of God

If we have heard the voice of God,
may our hearts be open and true.

Come and sing songs to God;
let us shout, dance and sing praise
to the rock who saves us!
Enter God's house with joy,
with music let us sing!

Let us kneel and give worship to God.
God is the one who made us,
and we are the chosen people,
tended like sheep by their shepherd.

If we would only listen to God's voice:
"Keep your hearts open and free,
as on the day when your
ancestors tempted me."

If we have heard the voice of God,
may our hearts be open and true.

Adapted from Psalm 95:1-2, 6-9

Sing Everywhere

Sing everywhere!
Sing of the wonder of God!

Sing new songs to God;
everybody sing!
Never stop singing of God's many blessings!

Every day,
move to the rhythm of salvation,
and share it with everyone!

Give to our God our deepest energy
in proclaiming this wonderful news;
our God deserves our praise!

Worship God
and blanket our joy with the best!
Be open to the power of God;
give thanks to the name of names!

Sing everywhere!
Sing of the wonder of God!

Adapted from Psalm 96:1-3, 7-10

We Will Walk in the Light

We will walk in the light,
for God is born to us once again!

Name God as our leader!
Let all creation share the joy;
the heavens sing the melody of justice
that will glorify all people!

Only the just will see the light;
only the pure of heart will hear the music.
Rejoice and be glad,
and may our lives be filled with
thanksgiving!

We will walk in the light,
for God is born to us once again!

Adapted from Psalm 97:1, 6, 11-12

God's Power Is Everywhere

God's power is everywhere!

Keep the music fresh and new,
for we have the wonder of God to sing about.
Victory is ours!

God's salvation is not kept a secret:
The gift has been shared with everyone,
the gift of forgiveness and fidelity.

Break into song and dance!
Every corner of the earth feels God's power!

Sing your praise;
pluck the strings,
and let the trumpets and horns blow loudly,
before the one who calls us all to follow!

God's power is everywhere!

Adapted from Psalm 98:1-6

We Are the People of God

We are the people of God!

Cry out!
Sing out to our God!
All the earth,
all the heavens,
cry out to God!
Serve God with all the goodness you can find,
and come forward singing for joy!

We know and believe that the Lord is our God,
this God made us well,
and we belong to the sheepfold,
the flock, for we are God's people!

March forward into the gates,
singing and dancing your thanks!
Blessing and glory be to God's name!

Our God is so good,
mercy and compassion are unending,
for we have a God who will walk with us
forever!

We are the people of God!

Adapted from Psalm 100

Our God Is Kind and Merciful

Our God is kind and merciful.
I will bless God from the depth of my soul!

Now with all my being,
bless the holy name of God!
I will bless the name of God,
forgetting not the benefits
and always remembering God's faithfulness.

Bless God,
who forgives our offenses
and heals all our ills.
Bless God,
who redeems us from destruction
and crowns us with compassion.

Our God is "mercy" and "graciousness,"
abounding in love!
Our God is a tender God,
not haunting us with our sins.
We are named "no longer abandoned,"
our God has come to save us all!

As the east is from the west,
God will come and cast away
our guilt and shame;
with tenderness,
as parents to their children,
there is healing and compassion
for those who fear God.

Our God is kind and merciful.
I will bless God from the depth of my soul!

Adapted from Psalm 103:1-4, 8, 10, 12-13

Renew the Earth

Renew the earth,
and fill us with your spirit, O God!

Bless you God,
with all my soul!
You are the beginning of so many things,
the earth is filled with your many creations.

If you take away the breath of life,
we perish and die.
When you send the wind of your spirit,
we become new again,
and the earth is renewed in your splendor.

May your glory go onward forever;
rejoicing in all you have made!
I am filled to the brim
when I meditate upon you;
I will sing of my happiness in you,
my God!

Renew the earth,
and fill us with your spirit, O God!

Adapted from Psalm 104:1, 24, 29-31, 34

You Will Keep Your Promise

You will keep your promise forever.

I thank you with all my being,
in the presence
of the community of believers.
Your ways are indescribable to me,
beautiful and exquisite.

You are merciful and kind,
you feed us well,
and we honor you.

You have showered us with liberation;
you have sealed your Word;
your name is holy forever!

You will keep your promise forever.

Adapted from Psalm 111:1-2, 4-5, 9-10

70 We Will Live by God's Command

We will live by God's command
and dwell in the blessing of God!

I delight in the commands of God,
for these are the ways
that the earth will follow,
filled with unending blessings!

Our homes will then be blessed abundantly,
and we will be lavished with God's generosity!
We will walk in the light
and be God's beacon of mercy and peace!

The poor will be covered in love
and filled with goodness.
The horn of God will blast in glory,
trumpeting the ways of God!

We will live by God's command
and dwell in the blessing of God!

Adapted from Psalm 112:1-4, 7-9

Our God Is a Friend to the Poor

Alleluia!
Our God is a friend to the poor!

All of you who serve, praise God's name!
Sing your blessings upon the name of God!

Higher than all things is our God;
God's glory is high above the heavens.
Is there anyone else like our God?

This God raises the lowly
up from the filthy dust,
from the stench of the dung.
The poor are lifted upon the shoulders
to be seated with royalty.

Women who once were barren
are now having children
and rejoicing in their new home!

Alleluia!
Our God is a friend to the poor!

Adapted from Psalm 113:1-2, 4-8

I Will Walk in Your Presence

I will walk in your presence, God,
in the place where you live.

How can I possibly
give a worthy thanksgiving back to God?
God has done so much for me.
I will lift up the cup of salvation
and call out God's name.

God holds all of us as precious,
if we die in faithfulness.
O God,
I am your faithful servant,
and you have given me freedom.

To you God,
I will sing my thanks
and make music to your name.
You are the promise,
and how I love your name!

I will walk in your presence, God,
in the place where you live.

Adapted from Psalm 116

Go Out Into the World

Go out into the world
and share the Good News of God!

Every country,
every land,
praise God always!
Lavish our God with glory!

God's love is faithful,
lasting forever!

Go out into the world
and share the Good News of God!

Adapted from Psalm 117

74 This Day Was Made by God

This day was made by God;
let us sing and rejoice forever!

Praise God who is always good;
  God will always be true!
Let Israel shout forever,
  God will always be true!

The right hand of God is our power
and lifted high above the nations.
I did not die:
I am still here
to sing of the wonderful gifts of God!

The stone rejected
has become the cornerstone;
believe it or not,
this is from God!
Our eyes are dazzled by this sight!

This day was made by God;
let us sing and rejoice forever!

Adapted from Psalm 118:1-2, 16-17, 22-23

God Is My Help

God is my help, the maker of all creation.

My eyes are lifted high to your mountain;
where is your help?
It is from you,
the one who gave birth
to the heavens and the earth.

May my foot not slip under your guidance;
do not fall asleep to my needs.
I know you do not sleep,
you are always there,
by my side.

You are my watchtower;
you give shade to me when I am weary,
and again,
you never leave me.
I know that in your care,
the sun cannot pierce my skin,
nor the moon be able to chill me.

You keep me safe,
guarding and guiding me.
Whenever I come and go,
you walk with me always.

God is my help, the maker of all creation.

Adapted from Psalm 121

76 I Was Glad

I was glad when they said to me:
"Let us go to the house of God!"

We are near your gates,
standing near to you,
O Jerusalem.

Your city is strongly built,
and it is here
where we climb upward as the tribe of God.
For here are the places of judgment
in the house of David.

Pray for peace,
O Jerusalem!
May you grow with those who love you;
may peace be in your home,
quiet and security within your walls.

For the sake of my family and friends,
may I say: "Peace to all of you."
For the good of God's house,
I will work for what is good for all of you.

I was glad when they said to me:
"Let us go to the house of God!"

Adapted from Psalm 122

I Am Fixed on You

I am fixed on you,
hoping in your mercy.

My eyes are looking upward to you,
there in the heavens,
as a slave looks toward the master.

As a maidservant follows
the wish of her mistress,
so my eyes are on you,
relying on your forgiveness.

Show your compassion,
for I am filled with shame;
my soul is battered
with the mockery
and hateful ways of the proud.

I am fixed on you,
hoping in your mercy.

Adapted from Psalm 123

Our Dream Has Come True

Our dream has come true!
You have called us home!

When you brought us back,
we thought we were in a mirage.
Then we realized that it was true!
We could not stop the singing and dancing!

Others have seen us
and talked about you and your way with us.
You have been wonderful to us,
and we rejoice in you!

Restore our treasures,
like the winds in the desert.
If we dwell in our tears,
we will come back rejoicing,
laughing and singing:
"Our God is freedom!"

Our dream has come true!
You have called us home!

Adapted from Psalm 126

Happy Are We Who Honor You

Happy are we who honor you
and walk by your side.

We shall feast upon our good works,
and we will be in the favor of God.

Your beloved will be like a beautiful vine;
your home will be filled with children,
like olive plants,
blooming and dancing around your table!

If we honor you,
we will know your generosity
all the days of our life.

Happy are we who honor you
and walk by your side.

Adapted from Psalm 128

80 Our God Will Always Be Faithful

Our God will always be faithful,
full of mercy and redemption.

From the bottom of the pit
I cry to you;
God, listen to me!
Be sensitive,
and consider my plea for forgiveness.

God, if you keep an accounting of wrongs,
who will be able to face you?
But we know you
to be forgiveness and mercy,
that we may always bless you.

I trust you;
I trust your Word.
I wait for you,
as the guard keeps watch for the morning.

You will always be faithful,
and you will never cease to forgive us.
You will save us all from our sins.

Our God will always be faithful,
full of mercy and redemption.

Adapted from Psalm 130

I Have Found My Peace

I have found my peace,
for I have found you, O God.

God,
my heart is not filled with pride,
nor do my eyes
seek to see beyond my means;
I do not possess anything of greatness,
nor things beyond my reach.

I am still and quiet,
as a mother holds her child.

I have found my peace,
for I have found you, my God.

Adapted from Psalm 131:1-2

82 Everlasting Grace Is Yours

Everlasting grace is yours!

Give thanks to you, our God of goodness,
  everlasting grace is yours!
Give thanks to you, the God beyond all gods,
  everlasting grace is yours!
You alone are wonderful and mighty,
  everlasting grace is yours!
You created the heavens in wisdom,
  everlasting grace is yours!
You stretched the earth over and around
    the sea,
  everlasting grace is yours!
You are the source of all light,
  everlasting grace is yours!
You are the sun who rules the day,
  everlasting grace is yours!
You are the moon and stars who brighten
    the night,
  everlasting grace is yours!
You struck down the tyrants of Egypt,
  everlasting grace is yours!
You freed your people from the terror of prison,
  everlasting grace is yours!

You are the strong arm of life,
everlasting grace is yours!
You split the Red Sea in two,
everlasting grace is yours!
You led the people to walk on dry ground,
everlasting grace is yours!
You lead us through the torrents of the water,
everlasting grace is yours!
You toss the armies into the sea,
everlasting grace is yours!
You have struck down the mighty,
everlasting grace is yours!
You have rescued us from oppression,
everlasting grace is yours!
You who feed each and every creature,
everlasting grace is yours!
You, our God of all of the heavens,
everlasting grace is yours!

Adapted from Psalm 136

Silence My Voice

Silence my voice,
if I ever forget you.

By the waters of Babylon,
we sat down
and wept when we remembered Zion.
On that land we laid down our harps.

Those who imprisoned us tortured
us over and over again,
teasing us to sing a joyous song:
"Sing for us your songs of Zion!"

How could we sing these songs,
in this desolate place?
If I forget you, O Jerusalem,
may my right hand shrivel up;
let my tongue stick to the roof of my mouth.

Silence my voice,
if I ever forget you.

Adapted from Psalm 137:1-6

With the angels I will sing to you, my God.

I thank you,
for you have heard the words
coming forth from my mouth;
with the angels I will sing to you,
worship you in your sacred place
and give you thanks.

Because of your mercy,
your promise is good news to us.
When I called,
you answered;
you helped me remain strong.

All of the earth will thank you
when they hear your voice;
they will sing forever to you:
"Glory! Glory!"

You are the one who saves.
You will complete
what you have done for me;
for your love is forever!

With the angels I will sing to you, my God.

Adapted from Psalm 138:1-5, 7-8

86 **You Have Searched Me**

You have searched me,
and you know me.

God,
you have probed me deeply,
and you know me well;
you know everything:
when I sit,
when I stand,
and you know all my thoughts.

You know where I am going;
and you are with me at my times of rest,
you know me through and through.

Even before I speak,
you know exactly what I am going to say.
Behind me and before me,
you fence me in
and rest your hand upon me.

Your knowledge of me
is too awesome to take in,
too great to understand.

You have searched me,
and you know me.

Adapted from Psalm 139:1-6

I Will Always Sing to You

I will always sing to you,
forever and ever!

I will lift you high,
my hero,
and bless your name forever.
Every day,
I will sing and dance your praise!

You are mercy and grace,
anger is not your nature,
and you are determined to forgive us.
You are gracious to absolutely everyone!

All of creation sings in gratitude,
and the faithful ones bless you.
Let them share of your power,
let all know of your wonderful power!

You always are true to your promises,
and you are generous to all you have created.
You support and lift up all who have fallen
and raise those who hold their heads in shame.

I will always sing to you,
forever and ever!

Adapted from Psalm 145:1-2, 8-11, 13-14

88 **Save Us, God**

Save us, God;
come to us and save us!

You are always keeping the faith
and granting freedom to those encamped,
giving the hungry food and nourishment.

The blind can see,
the lowly are raised high,
and the strangers
are welcomed into your grace.

You sustain all those who are without,
but abandon those who walk the way of evil.
You will reign forever,
through all generations, you lead us!

Save us, God;
come to us and save us!

Adapted from Psalm 146:6-10

Everything With Breath

Everything with breath,
praise God with all your might!

Sing praise from the high heavens,
sing praise from the highest places!
All angels, sing praise!
All power and glory sing praise!

Sing praise, all you who govern and lead!
Everyone, sing praise!
Young men and women, praise God!
All ages, praise!

Sing praise to the name of God!
Sing praise to the highest heaven!

Sing praise to the one
who has lifted the cry of all people!
Sing praise, all who are faithful!
Children of God,
praise God!

Everything with breath,
praise God with all your might!

Adapted from Psalm 148:1-2, 11-14

90 **Praise God**

Alleluia!

Praise God in places holy and sacred!
Praise God in the great tent of heaven!
Praise God, our hero!
Praise God, everlasting goodness!

Praise God with blasting trumpets!
Praise God with the plucking of the harp!
Praise God with beating drums!
Praise God with leaping and dancing!
Praise God with flutes and all with strings!

Praise God with loud cymbals!
Praise God with deafening cymbals!
All who can breathe, praise God!

Alleluia!

Adapted from Psalm 150

Liturgical Index

Ritual and Sacrament Index

Daily Prayer Index

Prayer and Special Needs Index